Fantastic
Filling Stations

Tim Steil
Photography by Jim Luning

MBI Publishing Company

First published in 2002 by MBI Publishing
Company, Galtier Plaza, Suite 200, 380 Jackson
Street, St. Paul, MN 55101-3885 USA

MBI Publishing Company books are also available
at discounts in bulk quantity for industrial or sales-
promotional use. For details write to Special Sales
Manager at Motorbooks International Wholesalers
& Distributors, Galtier Plaza, Suite 200,
380 Jackson Street, St. Paul, MN 55101-3885 USA

Library of Congress Cataloging-in-Publication Data
Available
ISBN 0-7603-1064-5

On the front cover: Lowell Davis moved this Phillips
66 station 20-some miles from near his old
hometown of Red Oak, Missouri, to his farm just
outside Carthage.

On the frontispiece: An array of old motor oil and
grease cans includes the extremely rare En-Ar-Co
and "Silver Shell" brands. These cans are from the
collection of Gilbert Michaels

On the title page: One of the seven remaining
stations similar to Don Stein's museum in Lafayette,
Indiana, this particular station is still standing in
Mankato, Minnesota. *Courtesy BP America Inc.*

On the back cover. Top: Sixty-sixes galore! This old
Phillips 66 station—replete with restored pumps,
signage, truck, and building—sits next to old Route
66 on the western edge of McLean, Texas. **Bottom:** In
the 1930s, oil companies turned to mimetic
architecture in an attempt to capture the
imaginations—and dollars—of motorists. Of the
eight "clamshell" stations that Quality Oil built in
and around Winston-Salem, North Carolina, only
one remains.

Edited by Dennis Pernu
Designed by LeAnn Kuhlmann

Printed in China

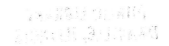

Contents

Dedication

To Joseph Anthony Steil
1914–2000

A man once accused of having swallowed a dictionary.
Thank you for your gift of words.
It comes in handy with the crossword puzzle.

Acknowledgments

Thanks to all the folks who went out of the way to help me track down pictures and share their stories. Especially Steve Rider and his fantastic postcard collection, Bill Williams, Terry and Jayson Scott, Marlene Wisuri, the Johnson family, Laurel Kane, Tom Westbrook, Lowell Davis, Annette Wagoner at Quality Oil, Tom Pardo at BP, Mark Quinn at Sinclair, and John Harper at Texaco. A big juicy raspberry to those that couldn't find time to return a phone call. You know who you are.

Special Thanks to Jim Luning for working cheaply, driving well, and repeated instances of unintended comedy. I won't tell anyone about the tarantula incident. Thanks to Bob Waldmire for the use of his spectacular art and all-around positive vibrations, and to Julia and Peter at Mondovox Design for last-minute Mac assistance.

Extra Special Thanks to Mary Alice, J.C., and Michael for putting up with it all and not breaking out in laughter as I walk out the door, disappear for weeks at a time to explore the backroads of our great country, and tell them it's "work." I love you all.

—Tim Steil, 2002

Yeah, But What Do You Call It?

Gas, service, or filling station?

There is a subtle semantic shift going on in America these days, and you don't need to beat the bushes for an English professor to get an example. Just pick up your local yellow pages and look under the heading "convenience store." Odds are you'll see some familiar names, including Phillips 66, Shell, and Chevron. There are still plenty of places listed under "service stations," but they don't offer much in the way of service these days. Wait, I take that back. The one down the street from here offers pre-paid cellular phone service. Sheesh.

An old, restored Phillips 66 fuel truck sits on display next to a filling station on old Route 66, on the western edge of McLean, Texas.

If you're of a certain age, or reside in one of those parts of America where progress works through the process of erosion instead of immersion, you'll remember a unique sound: two sharp metallic dings. Their closeness was a function of the speed you were traveling as you crossed the black rubber tube that stretched across the apron in front of the pumps. Typically, before the driver's window was all the way down, someone would be waiting for the inevitable "Fill 'er up!"

The windows were washed, and the oil and tires were checked. The restrooms would be clean, but not too clean, and somewhere near the front of the station there was a soda machine stocked with seven-ounce glass bottles. Inside, a few maps and cans of oil would be stacked in a neat pyramid. The men who owned and operated these places had their names embroidered onto a patch above their shirt pocket instead of a nametag pinned to the lapel of a company-issued smock.

Just outside Joplin, Missouri, old visible pumps help decorate a converted filling station. Although they don't sell gas anymore, from the signage out front, it seems folks can still get plenty gassed shopping there.

Allen "Pop" Johnson's Conoco. This old octagonal, prefab station was once in downtown Pontiac, Illinois. It was moved to a farm in 1937 and used as a brooding house for the next 57 years. Local enthusiasts stepped in and moved it to a park north of town, where they restored it.

Service stations were magical places, full of the sounds of dropped wrenches and bouncing tires. They were cool and dark, and smelled of grease and stale cigarette smoke. The coffee was strong because it had sat in the same pot all morning, and not because it was made from exotic beans.

Perhaps our nostalgia for filling stations has something to do with the smell of gasoline itself. Pungent as freshly ground coffee, and full of danger and romance. Even a faint whiff is enough to make the heart race. For most people, it is the most dangerous substance they handle on a regular basis. A fraction of a gallon can poison you with its fumes, or explode into a deadly fireball. That smell, whether it is wafting up at you from a hot lawn mower, or seeping out of the cuff of your pants, will take you places.

Pop Johnson was the last person to operate the station. He sold gas for 13 cents a gallon and had folks pay their accounts once a week. He cites a very good reason for taking over the business when he did: "I needed a job," he says with a laugh. Pops was tickled to see it restored, and donated his old Texaco uniform coat.

A quartet of pumps representing different eras sits in front of Johnson's station: a "computer," a "clock-faced," and two "visibles."

The Bennett Pump Company was founded in 1922. Six years later it became a subsidiary of the Service Station Equipment Company, but returned to its Michigan home base in 1936. Bennett manufactured "clock-faced" models like this until the mid-1930s.

In 1893, when Charles Duryea was still puttering about his Springfield, Massachusetts, shop building an automobile, gasoline was a waste by-product of the petroleum refining process used mostly for stoves. The first automobile owners were essentially hobbyists, much like these chappies who build ultralight aircraft in their garages today. The machines were noisy, expensive, and scared the hell out of horses. There was no such thing as a gas station, but a few years later when Henry Ford began rolling Model Ts off the line with a price tag of less than $400 each, all that changed. By 1920 there were an estimated 15,000 gas stations in the United States. A decade later it would be almost 10 times that number. The Age of the Automobile had arrived, and America would never be the same again.

In the early days, drivers had to plan their trips carefully so they would not run out of fuel. The gas station soon became ubiquitous, almost to the point of invisibility. In some cases they were tucked into quiet residential streets, hardly different in design than the bungalows that surrounded them. In other cases they were garish sirens beckoning motorists with a 60-foot dinosaur that towered over the pumps. Along the way service stations became an indelible part of our country's landscape, and burned corporate identities into our brains without us even noticing it.

While it has always been something of a second cousin to car culture itself, the history of gas stations, too, has been shaped by wars, political scandals, government regulations, and increasing concerns about the environment. What follows is a celebration of the ones that remain: the abandoned hulks on old two-lanes, the lovingly restored rarities, and all the others that fall somewhere in the middle. More importantly, it is a celebration of the people who keep these old beauties alive.

A classic English cottage-style filling station on Highway 25 near Orient, Iowa. Although the canopy and hastily tacked-on convenience store in back are new, the station's interior is much the same as it was in the 1930s.

Rusting pumps sit idle in front of an old station in the middle of the Mojave Desert. The fading paint on the front of the building reveals that it was also once an Italian restaurant called "Tony's."

While the stations themselves are impressive, the stories behind them are even more moving, and those stories tend to reveal themselves in the smallest details. In one station, nestled between old oil cans, is a jar of sand with a label that reads "Omaha Beach." On an old farm in Missouri, an artist restores a gas station from his hometown. In West Virginia, a man dying of cancer inspires one of his son's high school friends to restore an old Esso station. If there is a unifying theme here, it is that none of these people did what they did for a buck. They did it for a friend, for their community, or just for the hell of it.

15

Older than Dirt

Being a brief history of boss crude

Chapter

2

*P*etroleum and its by-products have been used for thousands of years in many of the same ways they are today. Records from as far back as 2200 B.C. describe crude oil oozing from natural wells all across the Middle East. Today, oil is an important economic force and military weapon.

Early Muslim historians recorded that many provinces paid an annual tribute in oil, up to 90 tons in some cases, to be used to light the lamps in the palaces of the caliphs. This crude *naptu* was also used to fill clay pots, which would be lit and hurled by catapult into approaching armies.

This old building in Bristow, Oklahoma, was a Sinclair Station throughout the 1920s and 1930s. It switched brands over the years but remained open as a working gas station until the 1960s. It is now run by Jack Smith as Bristow Tire and Auto.

The word "naptu" is a derivative of "naphtha," which is hydrocarbons that is distilled from petroleum, coal tar, and natural gas and used as fuel and solvents. There were even special companies of naphtha troops, known as *naffatun*, that would be sent to level cities that refused to pay tribute.

By the ninth century, the process of refining white naphtha had been perfected. In the *Kitab al-Asrar* (Book of Secrets), Muslim physician Mohammed al-Razi describes two methods of refining oil by using clay or ammonium chloride as an absorbent. The process was much the same as it is today, although the early refineries looked more like backwoods moonshine operations than the industrial behemoths we know today. In a simple, three-stage process, crude oil was heated in a lower chamber, the vapors from the oil would rise and pass through a condensation coil, and the cooling liquid would be captured in a vessel below.

In 1264, Marco Polo traveled to the Persian Empire and stopped in the city of Baku (now in Azerbaijan) where the villagers collected oil from seeps. The noted explorer was amazed at the quantity that seeped from the soil. "On the confines toward Geirgine there is a fountain from which oil springs in great abundance, inasmuch as a hundred shiploads might be taken from it at one time," he wrote in his journal. Although the Middle East probably comes to mind first, oil seeps occur all over the world.

A 1935 promotion from Sinclair Oil served two purposes: it taught kids about dinosaurs and oil drilling, and it kept their parents coming back. Twelve weekly visits were required to fill the album. Sinclair distributed more than 4 million albums and 48 million stamps. *Sinclair Oil Corporation, 1966. All rights reserved, used by permission*

If you lived
100 MILLION YEARS AGO

Sinclair began using dinosaurs in its advertising in 1930 and registered the Brontosaurus as its trademark in 1932. This newspaper ad from 1936 is one of many the company ran, and split the cost with local retailers. *Sinclair Oil Corporation, 1966. All rights reserved, used by permission*

Villagers in the Polish town of Krosno were burning oil extracted from nearby seeps in their streetlights as early as the 1500s, but the thick crude smoked terribly and stunk worse. In the mid-1800s, Ignacy Lukasiewicz, a Polish druggist from the Ukrainian city of Lvov, would change that.

Lukasiewicz had been experimenting with different kerosene distillation techniques, trying to improve on a process discovered by a Canadian researcher. Many people knew of Lukasiewicz's work, but paid it little attention. On the night of July 31, 1853, doctors at the local hospital needed to perform an emergency appendectomy, almost impossible by candlelight. They sent a messenger to bring Lukasiewicz and one of his new-fangled lamps to the operating room. The lamp burned bright and clean and impressed hospital officials so much that they ordered several lamps and a large supply of fuel. Lukasiewicz saw the enormous potential in his work and left the pharmacy, found a business partner, and traveled to Vienna to register his technique with the government.

Lukasiewicz moved to the Gorlice region of Poland in early 1854, and began hand-drilling wells

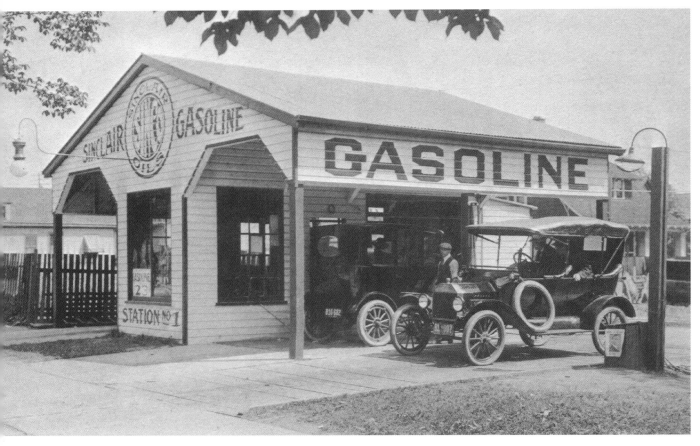

Sinclair opened their first station in Buffalo, New York, at the corner of Fillmore and Peterson. Gas sold for 23 cents a gallon. *Sinclair Oil Corporation, 1966. All rights reserved, used by permission*

south of the village of Bobka. He sunk several wells across southern Poland in the next decade and set up a refinery near Jaslo in 1859. By now, a full-scale oil boom was going, and today Lukasiewicz is regarded as the father of the Polish oil industry. He died in 1882, and 50 years later, a monument to his achievement was erected in front of the city hall in Krosno.

In the New World, the history of oil is almost identical. There is evidence that as early as 1410, Native Americans had been isolating small seeps by digging pits around them and lining them with timbers. In 1543 Spanish explorers used sludge from an oil spring near what is now Sabine Pass, Texas, to waterproof seams in their ships. In 1854, as Ignacy Lukasiewicz sunk wells in southern Poland, a doctor from Titusville, Pennsylvania, visited an old college professor at Dartmouth.

Dr. F. B. Brewer's family owned land near Titusville that contained an oil seep. He took along a sample of the oily water and showed it to his friend, who in turn showed it to George Bissell, another Dartmouth graduate. Bissell looked at the oddity and wondered if it could be used in lamps as a substitute for whale oil, which was becoming expensive. He had

During World War I, when most of Sinclair's male station attendants were called to fight, the company began using "Lady Attendants" like these pictured outside a Chicago station in 1918. *Sinclair Oil Corporation, 1966. All rights reserved, used by permission*

the oily water analyzed by a geologist from Yale, who assured him the stuff would make excellent kerosene.

Bissell quickly leased the land and made the rounds of New Haven banks. He received the appropriate funds and formed the Pennsylvania Rock Oil Company. One day, he spotted an advertisement for a patent medicine called "Kier's Petroleum or Rock Oil. Celebrated for its Wonderful Curative Powers, a natural remedy procured from a well in Allegheny County, Pennsylvania, 400 feet beneath the Earth's surface." In reality, the remedy was merely the nuisance oil that often seeped into Kier's salt drilling operation, and he had bottled and sold the stuff to make a buck. What stood out the most to Bissell wasn't the claim of curative powers, but the picture of a wooden tower that housed the drilling equipment at Kier's salt well.

Bissell assumed that if you could find the stuff by accident, you could use the same rig to get the oil directly from its source. He hired a railroad conductor named Edwin Drake to oversee the project. Drake went to William Smith, a local blacksmith, who was familiar with salt drilling operations.

"Uncle Billy," as he was known in the area, constructed a 35-foot derrick with a small steam engine to run the drilling rig. The locals thought Drake and his crew were nuts and called his well "Drake's Folly."

A year and almost $2,500 later, the well was only 40 feet deep and had yet to hit anything but water. Bissell's New Haven backers refused to give him any more money and leased the assets to the Seneca Oil Company, which, like Kier, sold the rock oil as a medicine. Uncle Billy and his sons kept on at the well while Drake spent most of his time fishing or playing cards in Titusville. By Saturday, August 26, 1859, records showed they had dug 69 1/2 feet with no luck.

The crew didn't work on Sundays, but the next day Smith was there straightening up when he noticed what he thought was water seeping into the hole they had drilled. Annoyed, he lowered a bailer down to start removing it, but when he pulled it back up, it was dripping with oil. He went into town, found Drake, and told him to come to the well. When they returned he told Drake to look in the hole.

21

Jurassic parking. Griff Westerman owned a small gas station north of this location in Lake Delton, Wisconsin. The four-foot dinosaur he had at that station was so popular he decided to use it again on a somewhat larger scale.

An American station in Baltimore, circa 1974. No matter what the brand name said out front, the Standard Oil torch and oval were instantly recognizable. The guys on the roof are another story. *Courtesy BP America Inc.*

"There's your fortune," Smith said.

That same year in Cleveland, John D. Rockefeller, a 20-year-old bookkeeper at the firm of Hewlett and Tuttle, borrowed $1,000 from his father to start a commission business with another young man named Maurice Clark. As the oil strikes continued in Pennsylvania, the two decided to get into

the act. Cleveland was becoming a major refining and distribution center for the Titusville fields. In 1863 the young entrepreneurs built a refinery with Samuel Andrews, who actually had some refining experience. They called the new firm Andrews, Clark and Company. Over the next two years the partners often disagreed about the way the business

was being run and decided to sell the refinery to whomever among them bid highest. Rockefeller won out with a bid of $72,500. He divested himself of the commission end of the business and joined with Andrews to form Rockefeller and Andrews, a new company focused on refining.

As kerosene use increased, John D. Rockefeller saw the possibilities in the burgeoning oil industry and increased his stakes wherever possible. In 1870 he and Andrews took on more partners and formed the Standard Oil Company. Their initial capital was $1 million. The new powerhouse soon gained control of almost all the refining businesses in the Cleveland area. A dozen years later they took all of their holdings and reformed them as one large company, The Standard Oil Trust. It had 42 certificate holders and annual capital of $70 million. In 1892 an Ohio court deemed the trust illegal, and Rockefeller reformed the different assets as the Standard Oil Company of New Jersey, where laws allowed parent companies to own stock in their individual entities. By the turn of the century, Standard Oil controlled almost 75 percent of the U.S. petroleum business, but a chance strike on a remote hilltop near Beaumont, Texas, would change the face of the industry, and the face of America, forever.

Wildcatters had drilled wells near Spindletop years before with no luck, but in January 1901, they struck black gold. It took them nine days to finally cap the gusher that launched the Texas oil boom. At the time, total oil production in the state hovered around 800,000 barrels. Over the next two years Spindletop pumped almost 21 million barrels alone. The area around Beaumont swelled with people looking to get rich, including speculators hoping to start their own wells and roughnecks ready to work them. Shantytowns sprung up as far way as Batson, where police simply chained troublemakers to a tree for the duration of their sentence since there wasn't a jail.

In the year following the strike, more than 1,500 oil companies formed and cut deeply into Standard Oil's share of the marketplace. Yet as the Industrial Revolution steamed on, public sentiment turned against the giant corporations. In 1890 Congress passed the Sherman Antitrust Act, a well-meaning but flawed block of legislation designed to limit corporate dominance. William Jennings Bryan, a populist congressman from Nebraska, was a fierce critic of the rich industrialists. In a Labor Day speech in Chicago, he compared the industrialists to hogs getting fat from the labors of others. "One of the important duties of government is to put rings in the noses of the hogs," he said to great applause. Editorial cartoonists around the country soon began depicting industrialists as hogs.

Ida Tarbell's landmark book, *History of the Standard Oil Company*, also turned the public against the company. Although she praised Rockefeller for organizing what was at the time a chaotic and disjointed industry, she also claimed he had used illegal means to gain control of it.

In 1911 Standard Oil was split into 34 separate companies. The Supreme Court declared Rockefeller's empire had tried to monopolize the oil business, but by the time of the decision, Standard Oil only controlled 13 percent of the market.

Rockefeller, who was still technically president of the company, had stepped down from day-to-day operations 15 years earlier and turned to philanthropy. He spent the last years of his life endowing universities, hospitals, medical research, and other humanitarian causes. Even today, the Rockefeller Foundation donates hundreds of millions of dollars to charitable causes.

John D. Rockefeller began his career as a bookkeeper making $3.75 a week. By the time he died, he was one of the richest men in the world. His Standard Oil Company has changed names over the years and been taken apart, put back together, merged, and purged. This Standard station was located in Minneapolis, Minnesota. *Courtesy BP America Inc.*

Fit for a King

One of seven remaining Red Crown stations and the man on a mission to preserve it

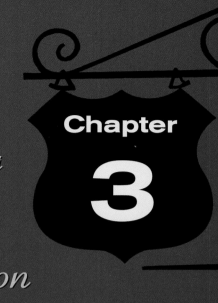

Chapter 3

It would be easy to drive through downtown Lafayette, Indiana, without noticing the little building at the corner of Sixth and South Streets. Set back from the road and typically obscured by the cars owned by patrons of the library next door, it blends easily into the streetscape. The former Red Crown station is an architectural rarity, and is one of seven left in the world. It spent most of its existence as a filling station before its conversion to a detailing shop and, sadly, a squat for the homeless. If it wasn't for the foresight and incredible generosity of a local businessman, it would be a parking lot today.

Clyde Jones ran the old Red Crown Station in Lafayette, Indiana, for more than 40 years. It was a derelict, ready for the wrecking ball, when Don Stein stepped in to save it.

The station was built over the winter of 1927 and 1928 by Standard Oil of Indiana, which owned the Red Crown brand. Many stations boasted a glazed brick facade, but since the brick company was located in nearby Attica and the delivery cost was cheap, Standard used glazed brick on all four sides, inside and out. The roof was covered with red tiles that were so expensive they were only used on one more station in the area.

Robert Graham operated the station for its first seven years, until the Walter Gray Chrysler-Plymouth dealership decided to

move next door. At the time, the station was situated directly on the corner and the dealership was concerned that potential customers wouldn't be able to see its showroom from the street. They struck a deal with Standard Oil to move the entire station about 40 feet to the southeast. In return, the dealership agreed to add an extra bay with a hydraulic service rack to make it the largest Standard Oil station of the 32 stations in Lafayette at the time.

In 1939 Clyde "Jonesy" Jones took over the station and, except for a hitch in the service, remained the owner for the next 40 years. Eight presidents and seven million gallons of gas later, Jonesy had taken only three vacations. By 1978, he was under pressure from Standard Oil to modernize the old building. He put them off for as long as possible, but the company cut off his gas supply because they were frustrated by his refusals. Jones closed up shop in 1979.

A local attorney bought the building two years later as an investment, but sold it to the Tippecanoe County Library four years later. They in turn rented it to a car detailing shop that closed two years later. After that, the old station sat derelict, and eventually become an eyesore and a hangout for the homeless. By early 1991 the library had decided to demolish the building and use the property as extra parking, but on April Fool's Day, a local car collector presented them with an offer they couldn't refuse.

Don Stein first came to the Lafayette area in 1949 as an engineering student at Purdue University. The 18-year-old native of University Hills, Missouri, arrived long on ambition but short on cash and put himself through college by rebuilding old cars and selling them to fellow

With a crew of friends and coworkers, and a "bulldog" of a secretary, Don Stein restored the old station back to its former glory in just two months—and for 20 percent of the cost "professionals" had estimated it would take.

students at a profit. Through the years he's become a successful businessman, and had a finger in a half-dozen or so companies in the area. He has continued to buy and restore old cars, and has amassed a collection that is the envy of many. He vaguely remembers driving by the old Red Crown station when he was a student, but he had no idea how closely he would be connected with it later in life.

"It just grabbed me for two reasons," Stein recalls. "First off, it was one of seven left in the world, and they were going to tear it down. That would have been catastrophic. Secondly, it gave me a chance to share my collection with the town, and the world." Stein went to the library board and told them if they would lease the station to him for $1 a year, he would

completely restore it and maintain it until there was no longer any public interest. He had a vague memory of the old building, but he needed harder details on what it was supposed to look like, and he knew just where to start: Clyde Jones.

"I went over to his home right after we had had a pretty bad ice storm in the area," Stein continues.

After the Red Crown was moved back from the corner, they held a three-day grand opening celebration and showed movies against the side of the building for all three nights. *Courtesy Don Stein/Red Crown Mini-Museum*

Stein has amassed a collection of rare Red Crown pump globes, including one that was illuminated by candlelight, long before the days of OSHA or, seemingly, just common sense. He says people often bring him collectibles they feel would be at home there.

Stein displays the two "Crown Jewels" of his collection inside the station's service bays. Next door, in the old Walter Gray dealership building, he has a few more collectibles, including a limousine that one belonged to the Shah of Iran.

"By this time he had to be in his late 70s or early 80s, and he was up in a tree trimming limbs that had been damaged by the storm. I managed to coax him down by promising him that if he would come down and tell me a bit about the station, I would send someone over to trim his trees." Stein wasn't disappointed. "He knew every single inch and corner of that place inside and out. He had an incredible love for that station; it was his entire life."

The library had originally considered restoring the station itself, but when a contractor estimated it would take over 18 months and close to $350,000, they quickly dropped the idea. Stein knew he didn't

have that kind of time or money to invest either, so he started thinking of ways he could do it himself.

"We contacted Standard Oil and they pretty much blew us off. I guess their thinking was that we would do a shitty job, and that they would get hit up for a touch. They virtually hung up on us," Stein says with a chuckle. " I finally got a hold of Lou Grad, who was a vice-president, and convinced him to let us into their archives. I just wanted to find some pictures or specifications; anything really that would help us. I finally hired a kid from Purdue one summer, and he went up there and spent two weeks plowing around these old documents, and he brought back worlds of information." But even armed with archival information from Standard Oil, Stein's biggest challenges were still ahead

"When we got it, it had no roof. There were a few tiles left, but not many. So I went to some tile people and they said, 'Sure, we can make them for you—$360 a piece.'" Stein recalls. "There are over 2,000 of them. So I figured, 'Well, we won't be so perfect, we'll make them out of plastic or wood,' but those people wanted a hundred and something dollars as well." Stein is a persistent man, and that persistence paid off.

"I have a gal working for me who is kind of a bulldog, and she started calling around. She got a hold of a fellow we had sort of befriended at Standard Oil, who told her he heard that at one time, these original roof tiles were stored at warehouse in Chillicothe, Ohio. So we found the storage facility and called this old geezer up, and he says, 'You damn betcha! We got rooms full of these things that haven't moved for 50 years. If you come down we'll load up your truck.'" Stein got in a truck and drove to Chillicothe that night.

"It was just a stroke of luck," Stein laughs. "Here they sat back in the corner of this huge dungeon of a warehouse—it had to be two blocks square. I don't even know if [Standard Oil] knew that they had them, or if the guy gave them to us. Hell, I could do seven more stations with what they've got sitting back there gathering dust." His roof problems were solved, but when he began to examine the glazed brick that made the station so unique, he soon discovered another problem.

"Back then, Standard Oil would hire teams of college kids to travel around during the summer cleaning and painting the stations," he explains. Upon closer examination, Stein realized there were 41 coats of paint covering the glaze.

Unlike its modern contemporaries, this old air pump outside the Red Crown Mini-Museum does not run on quarters.

"I had a professor from Purdue come and take a look at it. He said we couldn't sandblast it without harming the glaze, and scraping it by hand was also out. Apparently there was only one thing that would do the job—some chemical solvent that was so dangerous it was now illegal." Stein again turned to his secretary, who after several phone calls, located a few drums of the banned solvent.

This is one of the seven remaining stations similar to Stein's museum. This particular station is located in Mankato, Minnesota. *Courtesy BP America Inc.*

"I walked over to the police station, which is just across the street, and explained what we were going to do, and asked them to just sort of look the other way." That weekend, a crew of volunteers with army surplus gas masks worked around the clock removing the years of paint.

With the building restored, Stein began filling it with memorabilia, and a good deal of it came from Clyde Jones. His original tools and cash box, old uniforms, and the same clock Jonesy had watched for 40 years were returned to their old locations. Others donated items when they heard what was happening at the station.

Bear in mind, with "professionals" in charge, the job was supposed to have taken 18 months and close to $350,000. Stein pulled it off in two months with

When the museum was finally ready to open, Don Stein posted this short, but touching, note of thanks to the community and his family. He estimates almost 15,000 people a month stop by to peer in the windows and snap pictures.

DEDICATION
August, 1991

To the City of Lafayette/West Lafayette and more specifically, to the people of "the South Side" with whom I have worked diligently over the past thirty (30) years at Crown Laundry, Schnaible Service and Supply Company, Commercial Cleaning Company, Crown Distributing Company, S & C Realty Company and other business interests and who I have come to appreciate for their absolute dedication and desire to make this world better and Lafayette a better place to live. Also to my lovely wife, Lois and children Lori, Terry, and Todd who have aptly tolerated my idiosyncrasies, helped establish the latitudes to which I function comfortably, and reacted positively within the constraints of my particular personality and ability. This is my humble way of expressing my thanks to my family, to my business associates, to past and future customers, and to the people of Tippecanoe County.

Donald Jay Stein

volunteers and less than $60,000. When they finally opened, almost 25,000 people streamed through the old station that first weekend. Thousands more have come through every month since.

While Stein was, and continues to be, the driving force behind the restoration and continued operation of the museum, you almost never hear him use the word "I" in describing any of the work that went into it. He always opts for the more communitarian "we."

Stein's automobile collection used to total over 80 cars, but it is now slowly being given away to various charities. The most recent benefactor is the Imagination Station, a local children's museum. If for some reason the county library decides they really need the seven extra parking spaces they would create by tearing down the station, Stein is ready. He has set up a trust fund that will pay to move the station and its contents to a parcel of city-owned land, and endow it for 10 years after the move.

Modern Alchemy

Once thrown away as a nuisance, gasoline today is high tech

*C*rude oil is not much to look at, and contrary to popular perception, it does not always erupt from the ground in spectacular gushers, nor is one likely to strike it with a hunting rifle. Crude oil can be anything from a reddish liquid to a black sludge that seeps out of the rock like frozen mud. Raw petroleum is perhaps second only to water as the most useful natural resource the world has known.

It is impossible to look around today without seeing a petroleum by-product. The sneakers on your feet and the tires on your car, the rash medicine on your

Oil baron Frank Phillips grew up in the sleepy town of Creston, Iowa. After stints as a barber and banker, he founded Phillips Petroleum. In 1931 he built this station, one of the first in the state, on the western edge of his old hometown.

baby's butt, and that plastic thing in the kitchen drawer all have roots in crude oil. Even something like a hand-crafted wool blanket is made possible by crude, whether it is in the grease on the loom or the heat in the weaver's house.

In 1874 there was already a makeshift refinery near what is now Newhall, California. The little 15-barrel outfit operated for a just over a year, but it could never produce kerosene that didn't smoke in lamps, and finally went out of business. A year later, Alex Mentry moved his closed still closer to the rail lines and brought in John Scott, an experienced refiner from Pennsylvania, to supervise construction of a larger, 120-barrel operation. Their condenser at the time was a vast run of 1,400 feet of layered iron pipe submerged in water to help cool the gasses. The new refinery ran smoothly and pumped out non-smoking kerosene, lubricants, a variety of waxes, and a clear liquid waste product that was typically thrown away—gasoline. While wildcatters like Mentry and Scott can be heralded as pioneers, it was a mild-mannered chemist from Cleveland, Ohio, who had the biggest impact on the refining process.

William Meriam Burton received a Ph.D in chemistry from Johns Hopkins University in 1889, and went to work as a chemist with Standard Oil the next year. He quickly moved into management, and became a refinery superintendent in just five years. While Burton was an apt manager, he always kept a finger in the research he was initially hired to do. By 1913 he had perfected a system for "cracking" gasoline. Using heat and pressure, Burton was able to split heavy hydrocarbon molecules into lighter ones to almost double the yield of gasoline from a barrel of oil. Standard Oil eventually licensed the process to allow other refiners to use the same technology. Some historians speculate the discovery helped avoid

William Meriam Burton began working for Standard Oil as a research chemist in 1890 and became a refinery superintendent five years later. His discovery in 1913 of a "cracking" process that increased the yield of gasoline from a barrel of crude helped avert shortages during World War I and is still used today. *Courtesy BP America Inc.*

massive gasoline shortages in the U.S. during World War I. While scientists have tweaked and improved upon things over the years, gasoline is still made in much the same way as Burton's original process.

The first step in refining or "cooking" gas is separation. Raw oil is heated to a boil to allow heavier fractions to settle to the bottom of the furnace. The medium fractions, such as diesel oil or kerosene, hover in the middle. The lightest fractions—including gasoline—rise to the top, vaporize, and are collected in condensers.

The second stage is Burton's cracking process. Typically, refineries use low pressure, high heat, and a chemical catalyst to speed up the breakdown. The last step is treatment. Each oil company has their own brew of additives, from ethanol to dyes, that help distinguish grades to result in an incredibly complex substance. A typical gallon of gas contains hundreds of different hydrocarbon structures and additives.

Secret formulas aside, the cost of a gallon of gas by the time it hits your local station breaks down about the same. About half of every 42-gallon barrel of oil ends up as gasoline. According to the U.S. Department of Energy, distribution and marketing

A color-coded network of piping runs through these gasoline "stills." Although refining technology has been perfected over the years, gasoline, kerosene, and the myriad other petroleum by-products are extracted from crude oil in much the same way they were thousands of years ago. *Sinclair Oil Corporation, 1966.*

From cookstoves to fighter jets to speedboats, different forms of gasoline are used everywhere. In the summer of 1973, a Lake of the Ozarks water patrol boat gasses up at "Bikini Island," a floating gas station. Attendant Jill Phillips' uniform explains the station's name. *National Archives*

The earliest places to find gasoline were curbside pumps, but safety and aesthetic concerns soon moved them away from the road. However, in small-town West Virginia, it seems old habits are hard to break.

costs account for about 12 percent of the cost per gallon, with refining, federal and state taxes, and the cost of crude oil adding 14, 28, and 46 percent, respectively. Although it seems to sting worse each time prices go up at the pump, we still pay more for milk and exotic coffees than we do for gasoline.

Gasoline is like almost any commodity: the farther you get from its source, the more you pay. People in the upper Midwest have always felt the sharpest bite, and prices in California have always fluctuated due to the state's more stringent emissions laws. Fuel sold in California is burns cleaner than what is required by federal law, and there are relatively few sources of this exotic fuel, although neither fact seems evident by looking at Los Angeles on any weekday morning around 9:00 A.M.

It's safe to say most folks don't give that much thought to the stuff when they watch the numbers under "this sale" fly by at the gas pump. In its own odd way, that's good. Despite wars and embargos, oil industry posturing and increasing environmental concerns, gas has always been available.

While oil companies have always tried to build stations that blend into their neighborhoods, this Shell station in Cleveland, circa 1973, almost disappears. *National Archives*

In tiny Cerro Gordo, Illinois, Price's Service pumps nothing but full-serve. When owner Ron Price's old supplier refused to use gas that contained ethanol, he switched to Citgo. "Most of my customers work at ADM in Decatur," he explains. "They are the largest producer of ethanol in the world. It's just being loyal to my community."

Price's son, Doug, cleans windshields, checks oil, and pumps gas. This is a throwback to another day, and is an increasing rarity in this country.

Few people today can actually say they "ran out of gas" for reasons other than a faulty gauge or their own stupidity. The price of crude, while always subject to the whims of just about anything that happens in the Middle East, was just under $30 a barrel in 2000. That's up from $20 a barrel at the Pennsylvania Rock Oil Company, the first commercial well in the U.S., in the 1860s. If the tobacco companies had kept pace with the oil industry, a pack of cigarettes would now cost about 75 cents. Of course, if "big oil" followed the lead of "big tobacco," a barrel of crude would run you about $34,000.

Of the people who sit around and ponder such things, the camps are pretty well divided between those who think we will be out of oil in [insert guess here] years, and who that think we will never run out. The more pessimistic of the bunch like to remind us that, while we will eventually run out of oil, by the time that happens we will already have burnt a big enough hole in the ozone to have destroyed the population with sunburn and a flood from the melted polar icecaps. The optimists point to advances in the refining process, discovery of new untapped oil fields, and diminished reliance on fossil fuels in general. Regardless of who turns out to be right, the simple truth is "we" will never run out of gasoline. Our great-grandchildren may experience this, but their great-grandchildren are more likely to see the end of oil. Although it's hard to imagine a world six generations forward, if there is indeed a shortage of gasoline in it, it will likely be felt about as harshly as the lack of firewood for cooking fuel is today.

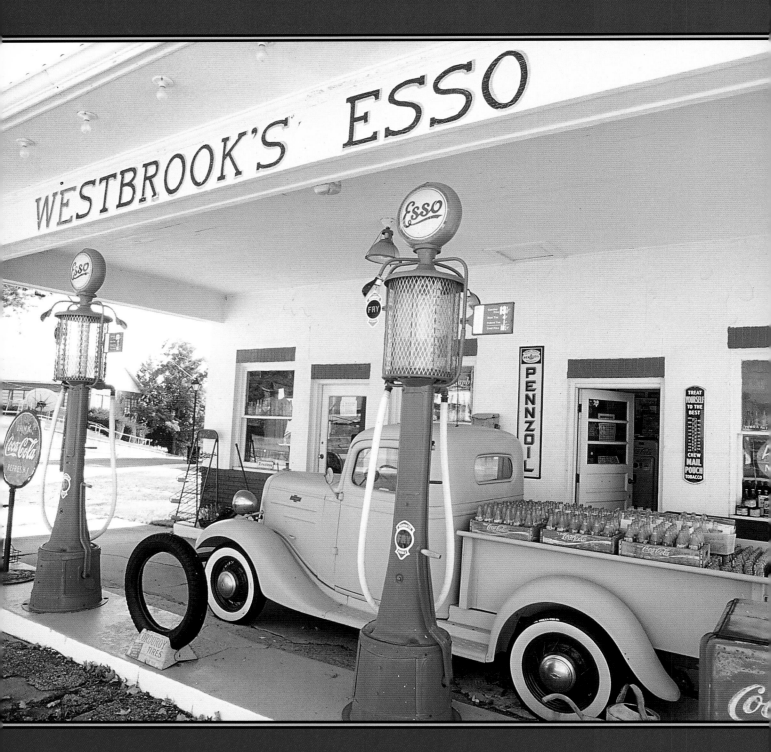

Westbrook's Esso

"I've known the history of this place all my life"

Chapter 5

$\mathcal{T}$he precise word for what Tom Westbrook is doing is puttering. The technical definition reads, "to busy oneself in a leisurely or infectious manner." Puttering is a behavior exclusive to the male of the species and confined primarily to basement workshops, garages, and garden-variety outbuildings. It typically occurs at the confluence of a lazy afternoon and a lot of small, none-too-important odd jobs. It is reported cold beer frequently facilitates this behavior. Westbrook sits in the cramped office of an old Esso service station just off Highway 7 in Kingwood, West Virginia, and shuffles bits of his collection back and forth.

In downtown Kingwood, West Virginia, Tom Westbrook added his name to the former Englehart and Loar Esso station. The two original owners bought the corner after being told by an oil company salesman that a new highway would be passing by it. Guess what? It didn't.

When he purchased the old building in 1994, he had no intention of restoring or using it. His main interest was the adjacent garage so he could have a place to work on his car collection. He soon found himself drawn into a project to restore the building, which has sat on that same corner for more than 75 years.

"The very first thing that was here was an old Gulf Oil station," he explains. "It was one of those old prefabricated metal ones with one pump. Then in 1926 they built this."

Two local businessmen named Englehart and Loar had bought the property after they heard a new highway would come through town and that that corner would be a prime location. As such things usually work out, the highway went through miles from Kingwood.

"Englehart and Loar decided to get into this because a fellow came through from Standard Oil and he said they were going to improve the road through here and this was going to be the new north-south artery. So they bought the corner, built the service station, and of course that never happened," Westbrook continues.

The two partners soldiered on as best they could over the next three years, but as the Great Depression began to settle over the nation, Englehart and Loar were faced with a painful reality. Tom Westbrook had been in contact with the Englehart family after he purchased the property in 1994, and wanted details about the building and its furnishings. One afternoon, while talking to Englehart's widow, she told Westbrook a story.

"When the Depression hit, the business just wasn't enough to support two families," Westbrook says. "So according to Mrs. Englehart, her husband and Harry Loar walked into this very office and sent the women to the back room. The two men then flipped a coin."

When they came out of the office, Englehart was out of the business. Loar paid him a fair share for his half of the station, and the Englehart family left Kingwood for Sutton, West Virginia, where something rather ironic happened.

"After they moved to Sutton, the Englehart family ended up opening two Esso stations, one of which that the new north-south road eventually came by," Westbrook says.

Harry Loar ran the Kingwood station until just after World War II, when a returning soldier bought him out. Over the next few years the business

Westbrook never intended to restore the gas station when he purchased the property in the early 1990s, but when Bob Hart, the father of an old high school friend, suggested he do it, Westbrook bit the line. The two men worked together until Hart, who was dying of cancer, became too ill to continue.

Harry Loar's Esso Station. Although he was originally partners with Boots Englehart, when the Great Depression struck, the business could only support one family. The men flipped a coin, and Loar won.

A Texaco fire chief hat and toy attendant are just a few examples of the collection inside Westbrook's station. Although he always keeps an eye out for interesting things, Westbrook doesn't place much material value in them.

changed hands several times, until it became Kelly's Esso in the early 1950s. That's where Westbrook's connection to the place begins.

"I've known the history of this place all my life I guess. I used to walk past here every day on my way to school," he says. "The high school is just across the street, and back then we had an open campus. You could actually leave the school for lunch and stuff if you wanted, so a lot of the kids would come hang out over here. Back here [back room of the station] they had pinball machines and a little lunch counter

where a lady named Mabel Leggett used to cook up chili dogs and cheese fries and things like that. Basically any kind of junk food a teenager would eat."

In the early 1970s Kelly got out of the business, and the station again switched owners and brand affiliations several times before closing for good in 1979. It was used as an office for a glass shop before Westbrook purchased it.

"I bought the place for the garage next door because I needed a place to work on cars. But then a fellow told me one day, 'You ought to fix that old service station up the way it was in the 1920s and 1930s,'" Westbrook says. The man who made the suggestion was Bob Hart.

Hart was the father of an old high school classmate of Westbrook's, and a classic car enthusiast. Westbrook had run across him here and there at car rallies, and knew that he had owned an Esso station in nearby Tunnelton, about six miles south of Kingwood. At the time, Hart was a year or two on either side of 70, and dying of cancer.

"Well I told him I wouldn't know the first place to start, but he had a lot of old pictures and things

Years after Englehart and Loar built the station, a garage was built next door. Tom Westbrook uses it to work on his classic cars, which include a couple of sweet Corvettes.

Vintage Esso Grease and Casite Sludge Solvent cans line the windowsills outside the station. Westbrook says he doesn't worry about people stealing them or vandalizing the place. More often than not, he finds collectibles people have left for him on the doorstep.

from around the area and said he would get me started. He helped for about two months or so, but then he became so sick…he became so terribly sick," Westbrook recalls, his voice trailing off. While the few photos and relics he provided were helpful, Hart's true gift was his inspiration.

"There were a few things he had that kind of got me started," Westbrook continues. "But for the most part he really got me thinking about the way things could have been, or should have been." With a little knowledge and a lot of enthusiasm, he began restoring the place in earnest.

"I just started going out driving around, and anywhere there was a pole like that on the corner, I would stop," he explains, pointing to the old signpost in front of the station.

"Even if it was obviously a residence now, I would knock on the door and ask them if it had been a gas station at one time, and if they had anything from that period. I would show them a picture of the station and explain what I was trying to do. That's how all this came about. I just started looking for things."

More often than not, the folks Westbrook asked would end up giving him something related to the station. Most of the things in the station were acquired that way. The collection is rather impressive, but Westbrook doesn't think of it in terms of material worth.

"When you get this much, you have to realize you have more than you actually need," he laughs. "I think the people who are really avid collectors sometimes get hooked into the idea of how much things are worth, how much they paid for particular items. They want to have the nicest example of something they can find, and I understand that. But for me, I don't put a value on anything. Even if something is a little beat up or rough around the edges, I don't mind. Especially if it came from here."

While the collection is notable, the restoration of the station exterior hasn't gone unnoticed either. Several racing networks have shot promotional material at the location, and the station was used in a 1999 calendar featuring old gas stations. As flattering as the attention might be, Westbrook remains ambivalent.

"It's had a lot of attention," he explains. "If anyone has asked to use it for something like that [the calendar], I've always said 'Yes. Just tell me what your plans are so I can keep an eye out for it.' But if I find that someone is using it for commercial purposes without my permission, I try to discourage it. I haven't really tried to commercialize it in any way at all. And I think it is my decision and my right to do that." In the end, Westbrook says, it is more about keeping the town's history off the auction block.

"I had a girl that came up the other day and gave me a deck of playing cards that had Kelly's Esso station on the back, from about 1960 or so," Westbrook continues. "Now those are the things that mean something to me. They represent pieces of history we can keep here in the community, as opposed to it being just one more thing of value that is being sold off to the highest bidder. Trying to keep it all together has always been my primary goal."

And now, even years after the fact, Westbrook still wonders about the fellow who started the ball rolling. "You know, it seems like it was only six months or so I really worked on it hard, and I'm not sure if Bob ever got a chance to see any of the fruits of our labor. I mean, I think he must have, but in those last days he was essentially housebound. You know, I'm just not sure."

Another Esso station is being restored just a few miles outside of Kingwood. If the work on the pumps is any indication, the station should be a showpiece as well.

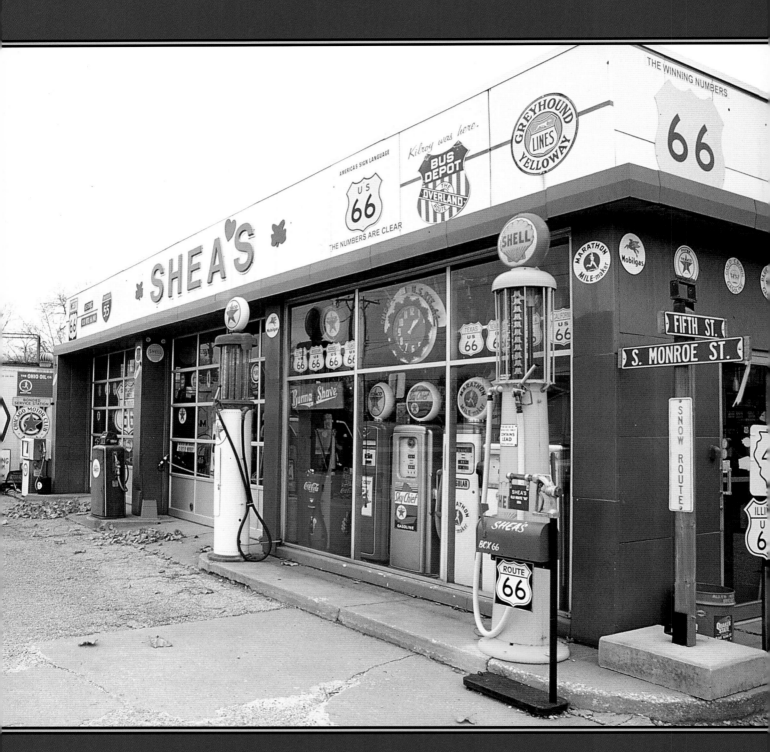

Bill Shea's Gas Station Museum

Chapter 6

"I'm pretty well satisfied."

Spend just a few minutes with Bill Shea and you realize you should have sworn boots—waders perhaps. The 80-year-old proprietor of Shea's Finest Truck Covers has a million stories, and some of them are even true, but you never know when he's pulling your leg, until you've been hooked, reeled in, and are flopping on the shore. Then you see that damned glint in his eye.

For over 55 years Shea has occupied a stretch of Peoria Street, which was once Route 66, in downtown Springfield, Illinois. Over time his old Marathon station has grown into a bit of a compound, literally packed to the rafters with

Today, it's simply known as Shea's Finest Truck Covers, but you'll have to pass through a mountain of memorabilia before you ever get to the toppers behind the station.

gas and oil memorabilia. While most of the serious petroliana collectors are happy to stick with globes and other assorted whatnot, Shea has added another complete station to the mix. This is impressive by any standard, but even more so given the fact he had neither interest nor intention of getting into the gas station business to begin with.

As a child, Shea spent a good deal of time hanging around the Texaco station near his home, and was befriended by the station's owner, Moise Deruy. "They used to call him 'Mud,'" Shea recalls with a laugh. "He had this French name, Moise. I remember one time a fellow came in and looked at him and said, 'With a name like that, you ought to be glad they call you Mud.'" Although he continued to hang around Deruy's station, and pestered the owner the only way a neighborhood kid can, Shea had no idea he would someday work there.

Shea was 20 by the time the United States entered World War II. He served in the Army's Fourth Infantry Division, and was one of the many brave young men that stormed the beaches at Normandy. When the war ended, Shea returned to Springfield and got a job offer from his old friend, Deruy.

Bill Shea moved the former Mahan's Station from Middletown, Illinois, 21 miles north of Springfield, and installed it in his compound on Peoria Street. It is rumored to be one of, if not the oldest station in the state of Illinois.

"Mud" Deruy was in his 60s by that time and hoped the 25-year-old veteran would come to work with him at the Texaco station, but Shea turned him down flat.

"He wanted me to go partners with him. 'No sir,' I said. 'That just doesn't sound like anything I would want to do,'" Shea recalls. While he had considered going to school to become an auctioneer, Shea had no firm plans for his future. After some gentle arm-twisting, he finally relented and agreed to help out at the station for a limited time.

"We drew up an agreement that we would try it for six months, and see how it went," Shea explains. "You might say it was a part-time job, and I'm still on it."

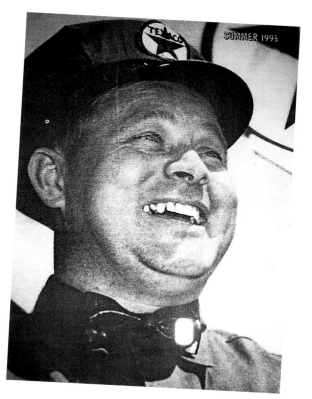

Before he opened the Marathon Station down the street, Shea was an award-winning Texaco dealer, and was featured in a number of advertisements. *Courtesy Texaco*

If an object has anything to do with a filling station, the odds are that Bill Shea has two of them. The most poignant display in his ad-hoc museum has nothing to do with gasoline. It's a small jar of sand tucked away on a shelf with a label that says "Omaha Beach." Before he got into the gas business, Shea stormed the beaches at Normandy on D-Day.

The newly christened Deruy and Shea Texaco served Route 66 travelers and locals alike. The two men worked 7 A.M. to 10 P.M. six days a week and traded off every other Sunday. The six months they agreed on came and went and Shea remained. Just over a year later, Moise Deruy died and left Shea in charge of the station. He ended up working seven days a week for years following the death of his partner,

Shea admits he's just about out of room at his station/museum, as evidenced by the ceiling. He's almost out of space there, too.

before he finally hired another attendant. He soldiered on as best he could for the next eight years, but soon outgrew the small Texaco shop. In 1955 Shea closed up the Texaco and opened a Marathon station just down the street. He's been there ever since.

They were halcyon days to be in the gas station business. In a prime spot on Route 66, Shea and his team of attendants and mechanics served untold millions of travelers over the years. When Eisenhower's new Interstate system began bypassing Route 66, many small businessmen along the old road began to feel the pall of extinction over them. When The Mother Road was finally closed in Springfield, Shea says he really didn't notice that bad of a sting. After

Shea was inducted into the Illinois Route 66 Hall of Fame in 1993, after 47 years of service.

Even a pair of oil-stained boots can't escape Bill Shea's joking. The museum is full of wisecracks like this.

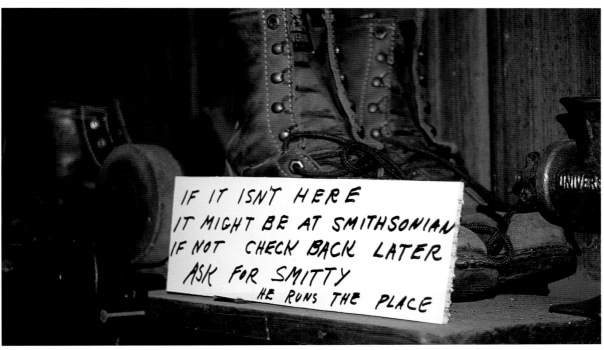

the oil embargo in the early 1970s, many people cut back on their driving, and bought tiny imports with double the mileage of their old cars.

"It was the first of February, 1977 here," Shea recalls. "But even then, nobody traveled the way they did [before the embargo]. Hell, people would drive 150 or 200 miles on a Sunday just to eat dinner. Going by here it was the only road, the highway that took everybody west. If you got off of that, you were pretty much lost."

Shea had begun selling truck caps, or toppers, a few years before, and was doing a fine business at that. As the number of gas customers fell, he finally decided the pumps were more trouble than they were worth and stopped selling fuel in 1982. Just over two years later, Route 66 was officially decommissioned as a national highway. Even though Shea's Finest Truck Covers no longer sold gas, it would still get the occasional tourist traveling the old road, who stopped by to snap pictures or chat with the proprietor about the old days.

Over the years Shea had accumulated a good deal of petroliana. When asked when he first decided to start the small museum, he takes his hat off and thinks hard for a minute.

"You know, it just kind of came automatic. I never really thought about a museum. Someone else gave it that handle," he says. It has become a museum all the same, and has attracted a goodly number of visitors each week. It's been featured in a number of national papers and magazines, and almost every book or video on Route 66. The museum attracts a surprising amount of interest from overseas.

"I think we've had visitors here from 59 countries," Shea says. "We've been in videos in Switzerland, France, England, and Germany as well."

Shea has this old oil pump hooked up to an electric motor and takes great joy in flipping it on as tourists passing by on old Route 66 goggle at it.

53

Get Your Coupons HERE

10 Gallons Gasoline FREE

Watch the Window for Lucky Number

IT MAY BE YOURS!

Drawing Every Monday Morning by the First Customer

Number Will Be Posted on Window for One Week   You Don't Have To Be Present

This Program Is Sponsored by The Management Personally

The "Ten Gallons Free" drawing was just one of many promotions that were used by gas stations throughout the country during the 1930s to draw customers.

It's a 14-by-14 foot prefabricated metal affair, rumored to be one of the oldest, if not *the* oldest station in the state.

"Some fellow had told me about it, so I decided to go up and look at it. But I couldn't find it—so many trees had grown up in front of it you could barely see it from the road," he explains. When he finally found the place, Shea knew he wanted it, but getting it to his Peoria Street location was a different matter.

"The floor had rotted out too bad to pick it up and put on a truck," Shea recalls. He went to a local welder named Dave Turner who surveyed the situation, built a custom flatbed trailer out of 30-foot rails, lifted the station up by its roof, and attached his pickup truck and began the slow run south to Springfield on February 26, 2000. When they finally got the old gem planted on Peoria Street, Shea, ever the wise guy, hung a sign out front. "Open Soon, Under Old Management. Hiring June 6 2000." The wisecrack and the veiled reference to D-Day would have pleased Harry Mahan.

Mahan was the last person to operate the station in Middletown and had himself moved it from another location on Route 136 near Knuppel's Corner. He ran it until sometime in the 1950s, when pain from a war injury made it hard to work on cars. The station sat derelict, and was used for storage for more than 40 years until Shea came the rescue.

While Shea has restored it grandly, Mahan's old station—and Shea's compound in general—are still

Although he has the usual array of petroliana—pumps, globes, signage, maps, and more—Shea's most impressive addition to date, is another station.

In 1999, Shea heard about an old Phillips 66 station in Middletown, 21 miles north of Springfield.

Shea and his wife Helen share a moment on an old bench seat inside the museum. She has learned to live with his tall tales and constant wisecracks.

works in progress, although Shea admits his collection is about as full as it can get. "I'm just about out of room," he says with a grin.

The man who didn't think he wanted to get into the gas station business has come to terms with the way his life evolved. "I don't know," he says. "I'm glad I'm where I'm at, doing what I'm doing. I'm pretty well satisfied."

Sitting on an old bench seat with his wife, Helen, Bill Shea does admit he might have done one thing different.

"I told this fellow from St. Louis once, I might have got up a half hour earlier every day. That's about it."

Posing for a picture, Shea looks at his wife, then at us, and says, "You know, these boys make over $200,000 a year doing this. They have a brand new Cadillac out there, and all their expenses are paid." Helen looks at him, looks at us, rolls her eyes, and leans her head against his shoulder with a smile. She's pretty well satisfied, too.

Hometown Boy

A Missouri artist's masterpiece, and the filling station in the middle

Chapter 7

Just outside Carthage, Missouri, is a veritable phoenix—a small town that has died and risen, died and risen again. It's been featured in everything from *Smithsonian* magazine and *Country Living*, to the *National Enquirer*. At its center is an old Phillips 66 filling station.

If there is any truth to Thomas Wolfe's statement "You can't go home again," Lowell Davis isn't buying it. He seems to be more of a 'bring the mountain to Mohammed' type. Although he is known around the world for his collector

Artist Lowell Davis rescued this old Phillips 66 station from nearby Avilla, Missouri. He first saw it when he was a child and traveled back and forth to Carthage with his family.

plates and farm-life figurines, Davis has spent over a decade working on a slightly larger canvas. It hasn't been an easy project anyway you slice it.

Davis was born June 8, 1937, in the town of Red Oak, Missouri, just off old Route 66. "It wasn't much really," he says of his home. "It was one of those self-sufficient little towns. We raised our gardens and Jersey cows, people helped each other, that's the kind of place it was. All my relatives were from there, all the way back to the pioneer days. It's kind of sacred ground to me."

Davis attended high school in nearby Carthage, but quit when he was a sophomore and joined the air force. After his hitch was up, he returned to the area and attended community college for a year and took a few art courses. He got a job with a local printing company and set up a small art studio to indulge his hobby.

Eventually, he received a job offer from an advertising agency in Dallas and left the area. He painted and sculpted on the side and received a contract from the Kaiser Porcelain Company in Germany to reproduce and market his wildlife pieces. As he grew successful with the agency and his budding art career, Davis tired of city life. He would often sit in his office, stare out the window, and dream of his old hometown. One day, he could stand it no more.

Davis quit his job and bought an old farm outside Carthage, just over 20 miles from what was left of Red Oak. He continued to paint and travel around the country and exhibit his work at art shows.

As he had the time and money, he fixed up the farm,and often rescued old chicken coops and sheep pens from other farms. When he completed a building, he went and got the animals to fill it. He began making sculptures of the chickens and other farm animals and his folksy Americana series took off.

"My line got very successful. My figurines were sold in over 2,000 gift shops throughout the U.S. and Canada, even in Europe," he says. " I didn't know what to do with all the money. I wasn't into Mercedes

Davis added a new roof and chimney to the station, which was falling apart when he put it on truck to move it to his farm off old Route 66. The unique paint job came later. "I just cutied it up a little," he says.

Where it all began. As a child, Davis first learned to whittle and carve sitting on the porch or in the backroom of the old general store in his hometown. He still goes there often to reminisce.

Cobbled together out of old sheet metal, "The Flying Crapduster" is one of Davis' favorite works at Red Oak II. Notice the old Rainbo Bread sign masquerading as part of the fuselage.

or swimming pools or villas in France. I had this big cornfield out here. It was kind of like this field of dreams. I kept staring at it like a blank canvas." Then he had an idea.

"I kept seeing my old hometown getting sadder and sadder. So I started picking up the buildings and moving them here." As the real town of Red Oak faded off the map, Davis began rebuilding it in his cornfield. He dubbed it "Red Oak II."

The first building he got was the town's old schoolhouse and, as he could afford to, acquired the blacksmith shop, feed store, school teacher's house, even the legendary Belle Starr's childhood home.

The most important building to him, personally, has been the town's general store.

"I was raised in the back of that old store," Davis recalls. "That's where I first learned to whittle and carve. The old timers would come in and sit around a pot-bellied stove in the wintertime and whittle and tell stories. I was just glued to these characters. I named all the streets [in Red Oak II] after those guys. When I was a little kid the war was going on, and it was just fascinating to listen to them discuss politics, or how much rain they had down on their place."

When Davis ran out of buildings in the original Red Oak, he looked for other old buildings to save.

60

"My favorite
art medium is something that someone else threw away," Davis explains.
He also has a sense of humor; like the tin can in the goat sculpture's stomach.

He found a gas station in Avilla, which is just down the road from his hometown.

"We had a pump at the old general store," Davis explains, "but there was no official gas station in Red Oak. Now, at the time, the big thing to do on a Friday night was to go down to Carthage. I remember seeing it as kid, the neon was just so striking. This was back in the late 1940s and we barely had electricity. Most of the homes still used kerosene lamps, so to see that neon was really something.

"I know it was run for a while by a fellow named Homer Hixon, then for years it was known as Knight's station," he continues. "But it was in pretty bad shape, an absolute basket case." Davis got the station for nothing, put it on a flatbed, and moved it to Red Oak II, where he started to restore it. "The patterns were all there, the awnings and everything, but I knew I would have to replace a few things. I put a new tin roof on it and added the chimney. I just cutied it up a little."

The real McCoy. The Odell station has been lovingly restored by volunteers from the Illinois Route 66 Association and with a grant from the Hampton Inn hotel chain.

The old farm turned into an attraction in itself, and Davis and his wife furnished the buildings with period décor and rented some of the buildings out as a bed and breakfast. They opened a small café and pub that featured live music on the weekends. He invited the people who collected his artwork, known as the Lowell Davis Farm Club, to stop by and visit his studio. It was a success on many levels, but it was a becoming a financial nightmare for him.

"This place was never designed to make money," Davis says. "Even if I charged everyone who came through that gate $2, I still couldn't pay the taxes. They went from $4,000 a year to $20,000 a year, just like that."

Local groups often rented out the compound for events, so when an area man came to Davis with an offer to buy the place and an idea for what he called a "patriotic Woodstock," Davis agreed. The 1998 American Heritage Festival was scheduled for July 17 through 19, and Davis and the man started negotiating the sale.

The event grew too big for Red Oak II, so Davis contacted an old friend, Sam Butcher (founder of the Precious Moments company), to see if he could accommodate the overflow at his 1,500-acre site in Carthage. Butcher agreed, but in the weeks before the festival, townspeople began hearing rumors about the folks who were coming to this "patriotic Woodstock." Among the exhibitors were supposed members of the neo-Nazi Christian Identity movement, militia groups, survivalists, and publishers of anti-Semitic books including *Satan's Kids: Facts Every Christian Should Know About the International Jewish Conspiracy*. Davis was shocked and embarrassed.

"Poor Sam," he says with a sigh. "I asked him if he could put a couple booths out there and they show up selling *Mein Kampf*." The festival went on as planned, and an estimated 3,000 attended over the weekend who listened to speeches and, at one point, burned a United Nations flag. Davis cancelled the pending sale, closed Red Oak II to the public, and, in an interview with a Joplin, Missouri, newspaper a few weeks later, said, "I want to apologize to the people of Carthage if I've dirtied their doorstep."

Two weeks later, the festival's promoters filed a lawsuit, and asked for $750 million in damages. They named a handful of people, everyone from the local sheriff to the publisher of the Carthage newspaper,

In this region, esp. along the R.R. tracks — watch for native prairie plants.

ODELL, ILLINOIS — This old Sinclair station, built in the early 30's, still sits beside the earliest 66 alignment, on the S. edge of Odell. This alignment was originally a part of Ill. Rt 4, which was created with the passage of a bond issue in 1918, & which ran from Chicago to E. St. Louis, roughly paralleling the future Rt. 66.

ODELL (Alt. 721 ft.) was incorporated in 1854 & was named for William Odell; downtown's beautiful old brick buildings perch on both sides of the railroad tracks. In addition to the old "city 66" align. which winds through the town, & this "early 2-lane by-pass," a pristine stretch of 4-lane 66 curves around the town.

OLD ROUTE 66 Scenes! ©1990 [2] by R. Waldmire

To Dwight
Old Alton R.R. Tracks
"City 66"
Odell
Old Station
First Bypass — 2 lane
Second Bypass — 4 lane
To Pontiac

Lowell Davis isn't the only artist inspired by gas stations. Bob Waldmire, famous for his bird's-eye maps of the U.S., created this drawing of a station in Odell, Illinois. *Courtesy Bob Waldmire*

and claimed that by spreading "fear, danger, and paranoia" about the exhibitors, they had violated their Constitutional rights.

"I shut it down," Davis says. "We had a big auction and sold off everything that needed upkeep. I couldn't sleep at night. It just wore me out." He moved off the farm to a small town south of Carthage, but he couldn't stay away forever.

Two years later he returned, slapped on a few coats of paint here and there, and reopened Red Oak II to the public. A couple moved into one of the houses and started an Internet business that they assured him would bring in money and help turn the place around.

"I got really excited about it again," says Davis. "I went out and started making signs and borrowing money to fix the place up. I gave them free rent and everything, but nothing ever happened. It was another lead balloon." Although the place is still open to the public, Davis closed down the pub to lower his property taxes.

"I don't know how I keep it [Red Oak II] going," he says. "I'd like to turn it over to a non-profit corporation or something. Maybe I can get a historic grant or an art grant or something."

Through all the ups and downs with the place, Davis has no regrets. "I never did this to make money, and it never has made any. I have five kids, and they all try to stay on the bad side of me so they don't inherit it," he says with laugh.

"I try to pretend the rest of the world doesn't go on in here. There has to be someplace where you can escape all the greed and evil in this world, and I hope that Red Oak II can be that place."

Davis often returns the general store where he grew up, and sits in the back and reminisce.

"It's a shame to see it falling down, but it's better than when it was so commercialized. I want people to see it for what it is: a work of art. It's my masterpiece."

But is it Art?

Many forms, one function

*A*lthough it's safe to say most folks don't pay that much attention to the design of the building where they fill their tank, gas station architecture can be surprisingly complex.

The earliest stations weren't much more than a pump and a small shed to house the attendant and a few sundries. They were often considered eyesores in the residential areas that they moved into, and to stay on the good side of their neighbors, the oil companies started designing stations that blended into streetscapes. Quaint-looking cottages, replete with cozy chimneys and window boxes for flowers, soon replaced the dirty shacks.

This Big Pump station was originally built in 1937 in Maryville, Missouri. A prime example of mimetic architecture, it was moved to the property of the Tri-County Historical Society in nearby King City.

In addition to stations that resembled houses, gas station owners soon found another amenity that was important to travelers—clean restrooms. Given the number of people who used them throughout the day, they were often filthy. When the companies realized customers, particularly the female of the species, found this intolerable, they began advertising campaigns that focused on the cleanliness of their facilities.

Texaco had its "Registered Rest Rooms" promotion and certified that each restroom was numbered, the dealer had taken an eight-point oath to maintain them, and a team of inspectors traveled the country ensuring their upkeep. Phillips did Texaco one better with teams of "Highway Hostesses," uniformed nurses that inspected the restrooms and certified them as being "hospital clean."

A clean privy aside, the most powerful factor in gas station design over the years has been that of corporate identity. From the

shapes of their stations to the various mascots, logos, or schools of architecture associated with them, big oil has burned their brand names into our consciousness from day one. Even with the company name obscured, the logos are instantly recognizable. Who

Buildings shaped like tepees are a common site throughout the Southwest. Gift shops, cigarette stands, motels, and this station in northern Arizona all adopted the theme. *National Archives*

66

The Beautiful GULF LIGHTHOUSE SERVICE STATION County Causeway . . . Miami Beach, Florida

This Gulf station, located in Miami Beach, plays up its proximity to the causeway with a lighthouse motif, another example of mimetic, or programmatic, architecture. *Lake County (Illinois) Discovery Museum/Curt Teich Postcard Archives*

could look at a red pegasus, green dinosaur, or yellow clamshell and not know the brand of gasoline that was being sold?

Yet for all the thought that has gone into gas station logos and design, and all the inevitable updates to them, there are still just a handful of basic station designs: a box with or without a connected canopy, an oblong box with or without a couple of service bays, and a "house" with or without bays or canopy or both. The one place where all these rules are broken is in the programmatic, or mimetic, school.

Simply put, mimetic architecture involves a building that looks like something else: a gas station shaped like a big gas pump or a restaurant shaped

Although the color scheme looks familiar, this Florida Amoco station appears to have fallen over on its side. *Courtesy BP America Inc.*

like a huge brown derby, perhaps. Sometimes the form was actually related to some function, but these roadside oddities always caught the eye. One of the best marriages of mimetic architecture and the retail gas business that has been found occurred in North Carolina.

In 1930, Joe Glenn and Bert Bennett took over a gas distributorship for Shell Oil, a fairly unknown gasoline company at the time. Looking for a way to garner interest in both their outlets and the Shell name in general, the pair constructed eight gas stations shaped like the Shell corporate logo. The stations were made of bent wood and wire frames that were overlaid with concrete and painted in the classic, bright yellow Shell colors. Although the stations built a name for both Quality Oil and the Shell brand, they were not as profitable as the company had hoped. Only one remains today, at the corner of Sprague and Peachtree, in Winston-Salem, North Carolina. The non-profit organization Preservation North Carolina restored the station to its former glory and uses it for a regional office.

The Koontz Coffee Pot in Bedford, Pennsylvania, served up cheap gas and hot coffee. This building is another example of mimetic architecture. *Author Collection*

Over the years gas station architecture has run the gamut of styles. English cottages gave way to Art Deco, and Googie was replaced by the Colonial revival. Along the way some heavy hitters joined the fray. Ludwig Mies Van Der Rohe built one of his trademark steel boxes on the campus of the Illinois Institute of Technology in Chicago. In 1934 Texaco hired renowned designer Walter Dorwin Teague to give their stations a facelift. Teague, famous for the Brownie camera he designed for Kodak and his glassware for the Steuben company, created the streamlined white station with forest green piping and stars. While more than 10,000 of the Texacos were built, another architect with three names designed a station that remains the most striking, and unique, in the world.

The Wright Stuff

One of the world's greatest architects and the filling station he designed

*F*rank Lloyd Wright is undeniably one of the most prolific and influential architects of the last century. During his 72-year career, he produced over 800 designs, more than half of which were built. His signature Prairie style featured long vertical lines, open interiors, and a quest for harmony with the building's natural surroundings. He built everything from coach houses to museums, warehouses to hotels, and all are immediately recognizable as his work.

Frank Lloyd Wright designed this station in Cloquet, Minnesota, as part of a larger project called Broadacre City. The only building from the project that was ever constructed, the station features a two-story office, living quarters, and storage space in the back. *Courtesy Susan Anderson*

Although hundreds of Wright's buildings still stand, the one at the corner of Highways 33 and 45 in Cloquet, Minnesota, is the rarest. It is the only gas station he ever designed, and is part of a grander vision of what he thought an ideal community should look like.

Wright first began describing what he called Broadacre City in his 1932 book, *The Disappearing City*, and continued to refine the concept until his death 29 years later. He noticed the cluttered suburbs that had sprouted up around Los Angeles, Phoenix, and his Oak Park, Illinois, studio, Wright envisioned a utopian suburb with houses on one- to five-acre plots, restrictions on how close together skyscrapers could be built, and a low population density. Central

to the design was the notion that everyone should own a car and, with that in mind, that gas stations would be an important component of the community. "Watch the little gas station," Wright said in 1930. "In our present gasoline service station you may see a crude beginning to such important advance decentralization."

Although Wright's vision of a low-density suburb is unrealistic today, many elements of Broadacre have been employed in modern cities: divided highways with limited access (Interstates), pre-fabricated housing, and large regional shopping centers (malls). As far as Wright's actual Broadacre designs are concerned, however, the gas station was the only Broadacre building to ever come to fruition.

CHINN'S CAVE HOUSE GAS STATION

BROOKLYN BRIDGE, KENTUCKY

OA3557

In Brooklyn Bridge, Kentucky, builders made the best of what they had and tucked a filling station into the side of a hill. *Lake County (Illinois) Discovery Museum/Curt Teich Postcard Archives*

The Tower Station/U-Drop Inn in Shamrock, Texas, is a stunning bit of Art Deco. The town recently took possession of the building and is restoring it for use as a visitor center and museum.

Daryl McKinney was a student at the University of Minnesota in the early 1950s when he first became a fan of Wright's style. "As he put it, it was getting away from the box, opening up vistas, and making the flow of daily traffic in your home more pleasant," he explains. At the time, McKinney's father-in-law, Ray Lindholm, was preparing to build a house and wanted to have Wright design it. Although Wright was already a legend in the field of architecture, getting him to do the design was pretty straightforward.

"You called him up and made an appointment and told him what you like," Daryl says.

During construction on the Lindholm home, called Mantyla, Daryl McKinney got to meet Wright several times and fondly recalls the architect's quick and acerbic wit. "When my father-in-law was building his home, it was first supposed to be built from stone, but he [Lindholm] thought that was too expensive. Then it was supposed to be brick, also too expensive. Before they finally settled on concrete block, Mr. Wright finally looked at him and asked, 'Lindholm, don't you know a banker somewhere you could corrupt and get the money for this?'"

When Wright found out that Ray Lindholm was in the oil business, he enthusiastically pitched him

One Man's Dream, Another's Convenience Store

Frank Lloyd Wright constructed what many consider to be his masterpiece residence 70 miles southeast of Pittsburgh, over a small creek near Mill Run, Pennsylvania. The home was built in 1937 as a weekend getaway for the family of department store mogul Edgar Kaufman, Jr. The home was christened "Fallingwater", and was the aesthetic and architectural marvel of its day. The American Institute of Architects called it "The Building of the Twentieth Century." The *New York Times* agreed and said it "summed up the twentieth century, and then thrust it forward still further." It also captured the imagination of a banker named Craig Harper. When he inherited a patch of land just off Interstate 95 near Stafford, Virginia, about 40 miles south of Washington D.C., he left the moneychanging business, and decided to build a gas station. He wanted it to look like Fallingwater.

He built the awnings to resemble the stucco terraces of Wright's masterpiece. He dropped another $20,000 into giving the sidewalks and fueling islands the color and texture of blue slate. He wanted to include a waterfall that would have run from the second floor into a bank of planters outside the first, but couldn't afford it. In the end, he spent over $2 million on the project, which is double what it would have cost him had he gone with a standard, cookie-cutter design. The gas company he was franchised with thought he might have spent too much, although the company admitted the building was quite nice.

Harper's dream and Wright's influence still stand. If you're ever headed north on I-95 in Virginia, take a quick detour at exit 143A. It's worth whatever time it takes. Sadly, Harper is no longer there. The dream and the millions he spent to realize it is now run by a family not even from this hemisphere who, when asked, had never heard of Craig Harper, Frank Lloyd Wright, nor Fallingwater.

Just south of Washington, D.C., a former banker pumped more than $2 million into this station in an effort to recall the sweeping architecture of Wright's signature design, Fallingwater.

Quality Oil began building these clamshell stations around Winston-Salem, North Carolina, in the 1930s. Of the eight built, this is the only one left.

the idea of building the gas station design he had used in Broadacre. Lindholm bit. Construction began in early 1958 and it took roughly seven months to complete.

Built out of concrete block, glass, and steel, Wright's design also featured cypress paneling inside and a second floor observation lounge where customers could watch their car being serviced, or peer out the back for a sweeping view of the St. Louis River valley. One aspect of his original design couldn't be used. Wright had originally stipulated the storage tanks be positioned overhead with the hoses

dropping down from the roof. The local fire marshal quickly put the kibosh on the idea, and the Lindholms went with traditional pumps. Yet the most striking aspect of the design is the cantilevered roof. Made of copper and looming 32 feet out over the pumps with no visible means of support, some early skeptics didn't believe the thing would stay up. The building team even used a special chemical to etch it and give it a timeworn look in a day.

"It would have taken years to get that aged look," recalls Daryl McKinney. "But it changed color overnight." The station was ready to open.

"There was a lot of excitement from what I remember," says Mike McKinney, Ray Lindholm's grandson, and Daryl's son. "They had flags flying everywhere and there was a clown walking around handing out candy, all that kind of old time promotion." Apparently that excitement was contagious. The station pumped 17,000 gallons of gas in its first three days of business, and that set a company record.

The Lindholm-McKinney clan has operated the station for 44 years, which has held up surprisingly well, according to Mike McKinney.

"A few years ago we did a major paint job to restore the authentic color. It had been painted white and with different gas company colors, and that was back when lead in paint was used," he remembers. "The company had to bring in some real experts to strip it and apply the new color. It was a costly endeavor, but it has been restored to its original condition. Other than that, it's just basic maintenance. It's not a museum; it is a functioning gas station and repair shop, but you can see the original cedar in the restrooms and office has held up pretty well, as has the original red floor."

The original cost to design and build the property was $75,000, the price of a very modest home today. As part of their regular financial audits, the family had the station appraised as a business. The estimated value is somewhere around $200,000, but when you add the Wright name and the unparalleled uniqueness of it as the

Holy Googie, Batman! A tricked out Sinclair Oil station from the 1960s, complete with white-uniformed attendants and futuristic pumps. *Sinclair Oil Corporation, 1966.*

only gas station he built or designed, that figure jumps to $500,000.

"If we were going to sell it to someone with a mind to restoring it properly, that's about where we would have to start price-wise," says Mike. "But it has been in our family for three generations. It's not something we've seriously considered."

The family has considered somehow letting the local chamber of commerce use the site as a combination office and gift shop, but talks have never progressed beyond the "what if" stage. Even with the obvious pride, respect, and sense of responsibility and stewardship they feel toward the building, the truth is they've been too darn busy selling gas to deal with it.

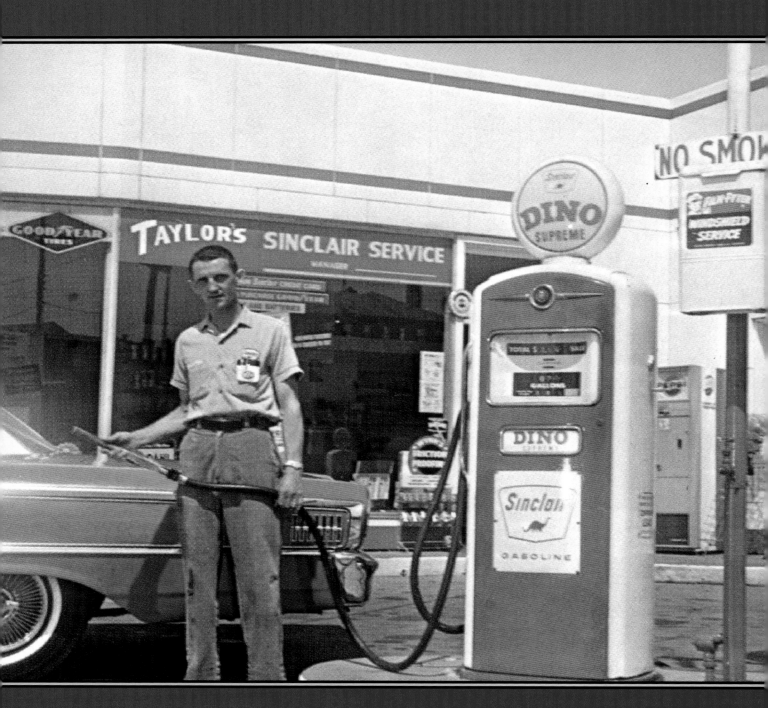

Hard Times at Home

How wars and political upheaval abroad affect the consumer gas supply

The oil industry, and retail gas stations by proxy, has always been deeply impacted by government intervention. From the breakup of Standard Oil to mandates for unleaded gas to a 55 mile-per-hour national speed limit, politicians occasionally feel a need to toss a few more regulations between a person and their automobile. Although some laws seem hard to argue with, others tend to sting. Nothing hurts quite as badly as cutting back the supply of gas available to the consumer, and nothing stops that flow faster than a war.

The halcyon era of American gasoline consumption—as illustrated by this photograph of a Sinclair attendant gassing up two tons of American steel at a Jeffersonville, Indiana, station in the 1950s—came to an abrupt halt with the 1970s oil embargo. *Courtesy Quantity Postcards*

While widespread rationing of petroleum products occurred during World War I, it was World War II that put the greatest squeeze on the American people. Even with adequate domestic supplies, threats of shortages still loomed, especially on the East Coast. Much of the oil supply still arrived by tanker, which was a favorite target of German submarines. On May 15, 1942, less than six months after the Japanese attack on Pearl Harbor, the U.S. government imposed strict rationing requirements for gasoline. Drivers were issued different classes of ration cards according to their perceived importance to the war effort.

–An "A card" ranked lowest and allowed its holder to three gallons of gasoline a week. If you were a long-time customer, you might be able to squeeze it to four gallons once in a while.
–A "B card" meant one was "essential" to the war effort, such as a defense plant worker. Eight gallons a week, give or take, were issued to these card holders.
–A "C card" meant a person was ranked "vital" to the war effort. Doctors and railway and transportation workers all received up to 20 gallons a week.
–An "X card" was the most sought-after rating and allowed unlimited gallons of gasoline. This card was reserved for police, clergy, firefighters, and volunteer civil defense forces.

If someone's line of work didn't fall clearly into any of the general categories, they could request a hearing before a local board. The board was typically comprised of a group of one's neighbors, and they usually ascertained the validity or absurdity of a claim with little fanfare.

After World War II, the U.S. auto industry entered a gilded age. Classic old coupes

Gasoline rationing had already been in effect for two years when artist Harold Von Schmidt made this 1944 poster, one of a series that reminded civilians of the sacrifices soldiers were making on their behalf. *National Archives*

Gas shortages and rationing aren't the only things that can put a station out of business. When Interstate 40 (pictured in the background) bypassed Route 66 in southwestern Oklahoma, this old Texaco west of Weatherford closed down.

and roadsters were rebuilt by high school kids. Detroit began rolling bigger, faster slabs of cold steel off the line as fast as the prospering baby boomers could buy them. Hundreds of thousands took to the road in search of America, or at least a couple of weeks worth of goggling at it. The Interstate highway system was a still a vague notion in the back of Dwight Eisenhower's mind, but two-lane blacktop stretched outward across the country. As the super-highways began to creep across the land, even more people took to the newer, faster, and safer roads.

Just as the Eisenhower era gave way to Camelot, a group of representatives from a five oil-producing countries—Iran, Iraq, Kuwait, Saudi Arabia, and Venezuela—met in Baghdad, Iraq, to find a way to control prices on the worldwide oil market. Their charter states that the purpose of the Organization of Petroleum Exporting Countries is to "ensure the stabilization of oil prices in international oil markets with a view to eliminating harmful and unnecessary fluctuations with due regard being given at all times to the interests of oil producing nations." It must have been hard to say with a straight face.

Six more countries joined the new coalition in the next decade. Once a year, the oil ministers would meet in Vienna to toss about ideas on production levels, re-affirm old agreements, and pursue new business. OPEC was originally a coalition of businessmen, but the Mideast was a political hotbed, and terrorism and border skirmishes were a common occurrence. The political views of the oil ministers would soon find their way into the group's trade decisions.

Even before gas rationing started in 1973, some stations were already running out of fuel to sell, as evidenced by this ironic photo. *National Archives*

82

During the height of the 1970s oil embargo, proprietors would keep filling stations open as long as they had fuel to sell, and then close up to save on payroll costs. *National Archives*

Shortly after the Yom Kippur War broke out in 1973, President Richard Nixon requested $2.2 billion from Congress to cover the cost of a massive airlift of aid to Israel. Incensed by the blatant political snub from the U.S, OPEC ministers demanded a 100 percent increase in the price of oil. Nixon Administration energy policy members backpedaled on the issue until King Faisal banned oil shipments from Saudi Arabia to the U.S. on October 19, 1973. The other OPEC ministers soon fell in line and American drivers braced for shortages once again.

Although there were no ration books to speak of, states began devising their own ways to slow the flow of gasoline to a trickle. Many states adopted odd-even plans, limiting how many times a week a driver could purchase fuel. Oregon came up with an alternative and used a system of flags to alert customers to that day's availability. A green flag meant everyone was welcome, yellow was for commercial vehicles only, and red meant no gas for anyone. Some stations sold imported gasoline at extremely inflated prices, but more often than not, they ended up losing money themselves because they paid too much for the gas to begin with and were stuck with it after prices fell. Drivers around the

A placard that used the green, yellow, and red traffic signal system explained Oregon's rationing system during the 1970s embargo.
National Archives

GREEN FLAG
EVERYONE WELCOME

YELLOW FLAG
COMMERCIAL
• TRUCKS
• CARS
BURDEN OF PROOF ON CUSTOMER

RED FLAG
CLOSED
NO GAS

country adapted to the new austerity with a grumble. The newer ones reeked with the indignity of it all, and those old enough to remember World War II were thankful that tires, coffee, and sugar were also not rationed.

The embargo finally ended March 18, 1974, when OPEC ministers agreed to lift the ban against the U.S after Israeli officials promised the cede captured Syrian territory. Five years later, as anti-American sentiment boiled over in Iran, another embargo was avoided. Many drivers, already steeled by the 1973–1974 embargo, had grown less dependent on gas and used public transportation or drove more economical vehicles.

Even today the oil industry is as potentially explosive politically as it is chemically. Every time tensions rise in the Mideast, gas companies get wobbly knees and wobblier excuses about the their usually immediate jumps in price. The day terrorists attacked New York City and Washington, D.C., panicked gas dealers in the Midwest jacked their prices as high as $5 a gallon. The Illinois Attorney General's office sued and won a case against one chain, the Iowa-based Casey's, and claimed unfair price gouging. It's a roller coaster that Americans are slowly becoming accustomed to.

It seems that the only things we can be truly sure of are that, no matter what any of the government types do here or abroad, the major oil companies and their stockholders will continue to reap higher profits, and when push comes to shove, America will be ready to send its military to assure the continued flow of oil.

An army might march on its stomach, but a navy runs on fuel. During World War II, a Sinclair barge loads drums of aviation fuel onto an aircraft carrier in New York Harbor. *Sinclair Oil Corporation, 1966. All rights reserved, used by permission*

85

On a Wing and a Prayer

"He bet him $5 he couldn't get one"

Chapter 11

For almost 60 years, unwary travelers along Highway 99E in Milwaukie, Oregon, have been prone to double takes and tapping brakes. Towering over a combination restaurant and catering business which was at one time a thriving gas station is an aging B-17G "Flying Fortress" bomber, one of an estimated 23 left in the world. As if its location and rarity aren't noteworthy enough, the story behind how it got there is the sort of stuff novelists dream up.

Art Lacey in front of his pride and joy. He had never flown a plane that large before he brought the old B-17 home in a blizzard. It almost cost him his life. *Photo courtesy The Bomber Family*

In *Sometimes a Great Notion*, the sequel to *One Flew Over the Cuckoo's Nest*, the late Ken Kesey wrote a stunning tale of an Oregon logging family. The Stampers embodied the very values upon which the United States were founded: independence, diligence, and a certain degree of indifference toward the opinions of others. No one knows for sure who or what Kesey's inspiration was for the book, but a veritable *doppelganger* of the Stamper family is alive and well just a few hours north of Kesey's Pleasant Hill farm.

There are few more pure examples of the archetypal self-made man than Art Lacey. His life story is vast and almost mythical in scope. Born with nothing, he was worth millions when he died, and he had achieved everything he desired and not a bit more. He was a guy with moxie. No, that's putting it too lightly. He was a guy with balls. Big ones.

Lacey was born to teen parents in 1913, and was taken in by grandparents who raised him as their own on a farm outside Parker, Oregon. The improvised family had little and drew most of their income from the logging industry. His grandfather worked the camps, and he and his grandmother served meals to threshing crews. Although it wasn't much of a secret, they also ran a successful bootlegging operation and claimed they could make better Canadian whiskey than the Canadians.

ART LACEY'S BOMBER STATION
The only one in the world--6 mi. so. of Portland, Ore., on 99E

An early postcard of The Bomber. When Lacey opened the business six miles south of Portland, there was almost nothing around. Before long, Lacey added a restaurant and six islands of pumps. *Photo courtesy The Bomber Family*

After serving with the Army Corps of Engineers in World War II, Lacey returned to the Portland area and opened a pair of gas stations, one at Seventh and Ashland, and another at Thirty-fourth and Division. In 1947, while sitting around playing poker with some friends at his birthday party, Lacey mentioned an idea he had about using an airplane as a canopy for a service station. Jayson Scott, Lacey's grandson, remembers the story well.

"It was a guy named Bob Harris from Harris Oil, in Vancouver, Washington. Art had mentioned this idea about using an airplane as a canopy, and Bob asked him what kind of airplane. He said he wanted to get one of those big B-17 bombers, and Harris said it couldn't be done. He bet him $5 he could. Then he got up from the table and left for Oklahoma that night."

Lacey knew that the air force had been mothballing World War II surplus aircraft at bases in Oklahoma, and headed straight for Tinker AFB near Oklahoma City. When he arrived, there weren't any planes around. He asked a cab driver who told him the bombers were actually at a base outside Altus, 125 miles southwest of Oklahoma City.

Lacey pushed on to Altus AFB, and after the requisite paperwork, he turned over $13,750 and became the proud owner of a B-17. He hired a crew of locals to help him "unpickle" the 18-ton behemoth and

Attendants at the station and waitresses at the restaurant next door were referred to as "The Bomber Crew," and many of the entrees on the menu had military nicknames. *Photo courtesy The Bomber Family*

Art Lacey's grandson spent most of a brutal summer cleaning the interior of the plane. When they decided to restore it properly, they removed the cockpit and spent $300,000 on the job. It's now on display inside the restaurant. *Photo courtesy The Bomber Family*

make it airworthy again. A short time later, she was ready to fly, but there was just one minor detail.

Base regulations required Lacey to have a co-pilot to fly the plane. Since none of the farmhands he had hired were remotely qualified for the job, Lacey had to improvise.

"One of the firemen at the base had a mother who was a dressmaker," recalls Scott. "So he went home and got one of his mother's mannequins. They put a hat on it and strapped it into the seat.

That was his co-pilot." With the air traffic controllers satisfactorily hoodwinked, Lacey leaned into the throttles and lifted his B-17 off the ground for a test flight.

Lacey had a pilot's license, but the ink on it was barely dry. He had less than 10 hours total flight time and no training whatsoever in the large bomber. While Lacey didn't know it at the time, there was one thing his crew had not been able to test on the ground.

He put the plane through its paces, and once he was satisfied that everything was working, he brought her back to Altus to prepare for the flight to Oregon. It was only then he realized he couldn't get the landing gear down. With no other options, he put her in on her belly and slammed into another B-17 on the tarmac. Lacey walked away without a scratch. Since there was little damage to the plane on the ground (and also because if the true identity of Lacey's co-pilot ever got out, base commanders would likely feel some heat), the air force wrote the incident off as "wind damage."

That night, Lacey called home and borrowed another $1,500. The next day he went back to Altus and bought another B-17 with the money. This time however, Lacey got a brand new plane that had never left the U.S., much less seen combat. It had cost the Air Force $350,000 to build this airplane. In a matter of days, he and his rag-tag crew had unpickled another plane and made her airworthy. He recruited a couple of friends from Oregon to come down and help him get it back.

Jayson Scott, Lacey's grandson, is the third generation of the family to grow up working at The Bomber. In Scott's lap is the fourth generation. Although Scott knows the restoration will take an extraordinary amount of time and money, he is committed to see it through. *Photo courtesy The Bomber Family*

Before they taxied out to the runway for departure, Lacey did something that some would consider insane. He took his parachute to the back of the aircraft, put it in a wooden box, nailed it shut, and swore to ride his plane into the ground. He had sunk more than his life savings into the project. The flight home would be another eventful trip.

They made it to Palm Springs, California, with little trouble. Lacey and his crew refueled the plane, paid with a rubber check, and began the second leg of the trip to Klamath Falls, Oregon. As his co-pilots slept in the back, Lacey followed the Sierra Nevada Mountains north. Then all hell broke loose.

Perhaps he forgot to check the weather forecast when they stopped to refuel, or maybe he did and just didn't care. Either way, Lacey flew into a blinding snowstorm. Although the plane had a service ceiling of 35,000 feet, Lacey had no idea how high the storm was and both of his co-pilots were sick. One had a bout of gastritis and the other a nagging toothache, both of which would be aggravated by the change in pressure if he climbed. The storm raged on, and even though he was surrounded by jagged mountaintops, he began to descend and tried to get under the storm.

Flying by the seat of his pants and disoriented by the storm, Lacey swooped lower and tried to find some sort of landmark. It almost cost him his life—dead ahead was the face of a mountain. He slammed the throttles forward, pulled the plane up, and avoided a crash by inches.

Lacey spotted a break in the cloud cover, dropped down once again, and tried to regain his bearings. He spotted a small town and swooped in just over the treetops and tried to see anything that would identify where they were. Shocked residents ran out of their houses and thought the plane was going to land or crash on the main drag. When the crew finally spotted a sign, it indicated they were above the town of Fall River Mills, California. They were over 100 miles off course. Lacey put the old warhorse back on track and followed a railroad line all they way to Klamath Falls, Oregon, where they stopped to refuel. Lacey also took time to call home and have his wife put some money in the bank to cover the bum check he'd written back in Palm Springs.

By the time they taxied out to leave Klamath Falls, the weather had cleared and the crew expected a smooth flight home. They hit another blizzard as they flew north over the Cascades. Lacey was unable to get the plane above the storm and flew the last few hundred miles to Troutdale Airport at around 800 feet. While most people would look forward to setting foot on solid ground after such a perilous and exhausting trip, Lacey took time to buzz a relative's house before he landed. It was his way of announcing he was back. With the plane safe on the ground back home, Lacey had to find a place to put it.

"He had the concept before he had a location," explains Scott. "When he found this spot in Milwaukie, there was literally nothing around here." Even with the plane and a place to put it, Lacey had another hurdle to jump.

He still needed to get the plane across town to his business, and the local authorities wouldn't grant him permission to haul such a huge load. In the end,

he simply loaded up four oversized trucks with sections of the disassembled aircraft and trucked it in one morning at 2 A.M. In the end he paid a $10 fine for hauling too wide of a load. The plane was reassembled and hoisted over the gas pumps a short time later and Lacey opened for business. A year later, he opened the restaurant next door. Once he was up and running, he sold off the other two stations and devoted himself to the new venture.

The place has been a favorite with locals and airplane and gas station buffs ever since. More than anything, "The Bomber," as it became known locally, has been a family affair. For four generations the Lacey family has pumped gas, washed windows, flipped burgers, and done whatever was necessary to keep the family business running, and live up to their patriarch's motto "You stick and stay, and make it pay."

"I started pumping gas down on the island when I was five years old, " says Jayson Scott. At the time, his father had launched a dental practice and his mother was the assistant and did everything from keeping the books to handing him instruments. While his parents built their business, Scott frequently found himself with his grandparents.

"They were extremely busy at the time, so instead of me just staying in a little room and them watching me, I would go along with them while they were working. That meant going for runs in the gas truck to pick up fuel, and different things like that," he recalls. In an ironic twist, Jayson Scott grew up working along side his grandmother, just as Art had done in the logging camps years before.

At the time, the station had six islands of pumps with a separate till on each. "To keep me out of harm's way, they would have me stay at a till and make change," Scott explains. "Typically, the other attendants would go fuel the cars and wash windows, and the people would run up and pay me. By the time I was eight years old, I was better at it than most of the teenagers working there, and was running my own island."

And so it went, through elementary and high school and beyond. Scott worked the family business, and returned after college to help manage the restaurant. Over the years, The Bomber has become a landmark along that stretch of McLoughlin Boulevard, to the point that even competing restaurants use it in their commercials, announcing their location in relation to how far they are from it, but the years also took their toll on the plane itself.

Art and Birdie Lacey were married on the Fourth of July, and every year they threw a huge party to celebrate both their anniversary and Independence Day. In 1993, as he was pressure-washing the outside of the plane in preparation for the party, Jayson Scott decided to climb up inside and take a look around.

"At that time I was looking to get away from the day-to-day management of the restaurant, and have always been mechanically inclined," Scott says. "So I talked to my mom and said I had to do a little more work inside. I spent about three or four months taking out old debris and wood. It literally got to the point I was cleaning it with a toothbrush. It was hotter than hell up there, sometimes 110 or 115 degrees, but I was having fun." During that time, Scott began to connect with the old plane in a deeper way.

"It had been a part of my life for as long as I can remember, but the significance and specialness of it hadn't been apparent. It became a lot more personal to me," he explains. With the same stubborn determination of his grandfather, Scott went to his family and said they needed to think about preserving the plane.

"We figured we would do it as we could afford to, probably over 10 or 12 years. It will probably be a lot longer than that now," he says. For years, Scott, with a little help from a friend who is an aircraft mechanic, has slogged away at the project. He estimates they have spent over $300,000 on it to date. When they decided to stop selling gas, they took another financial hit as well.

"We were going to have to modernize the station, and it just wasn't cost-effective anymore. We were a true independent; we bought fuel on the open market. There was a station up the street that was selling gas for nine cents a gallon less than we were paying wholesale," he explains. "Then after that we were forced to remove the underground tanks. That cost almost $500,000. So essentially that money didn't really go into adding to our business in any way, that was just to save the property. It set us back considerably on the restoration project."

As it sits, the plane is worth over $1 million and the family has been approached by people offering that and more. If it were restored to the point of being flightworthy again, the B-17 would be worth six times that amount. Although seeing it fly again is a remote possibility, Scott says that all the work they do is with that goal in mind. They cut no corners, and painstakingly restored things down to the last bolt and bit of trim.

Scott would like to get the plane out of the elements someday, but he knows the people of Milwaukie would miss it, almost as much as he values it. "We'd get run out of town on a rail if we ever moved this thing." he laughs. "I just want people to know that, even though this is a very long-term project, we are completely dedicated to it."

Although Art Lacey passed away in the fall of 2000, his spirit and determination are still evident. When his grandson first told him of his plans to start restoring the bomber, Lacey told him, "The fight has gone out of me. You're going to have to take it from here, little boy." And that he has.

"It's been incredibly time-consuming just physically doing the work. We fabricate most of the pieces ourselves. We are really having to re-invent the wheel in some ways," Scott says, undaunted. "But I like taking on impossible projects. I usually get them done, sometimes it just takes longer than expected."

And just for the record, Art Lacey collected on that $5 bet.

Index

**The American
Gas Station**
ISBN: 0-7603-0649-4

**Gas Stations
Coast to Coast**
ISBN: 0-7603-0740-7

**Route 66
Lives on the Road**
ISBN: 0-7603-0766-0

Route 66
ISBN: 0-7603-0747-4

Route 66 Remembered
ISBN: 0-7603-0114-X

The American Diner
ISBN: 0-7603-0110-7

**The American
Car Dealership**
ISBN: 0-7603-0639-7

The American Motel
ISBN: 0-7603-0101-8

**The American
Amusement Park**
ISBN: 0-7603-0981-7